EXPLORE THE BIBLE: Hebrews, Chapters 8–13

© 2014 LifeWay Press® • Reprinted 2018

ISBN 978-1-4300-3656-2 • Item 005693875

Dewey decimal classification: 227.87
Subject headings: BIBLE. N.T. HEBREWS—
STUDY\CHRISTIAN LIFE

ERIC GEIGER
Vice President, LifeWay Resources

DAVID JEREMIAH
General Editor

JEREMY MAXFIELD
Content Editor

MICHAEL KELLEY
Director, Groups Ministry

Explore
the Bible ®

Let the Word dwell in you.

Send questions/comments to: Content Editor; *Explore the Bible: Adult Small Group Study;* One LifeWay Plaza; Nashville, TN 37234.

Printed in the United States of America

For ordering or inquiries visit LifeWay.com; write to LifeWay Small Groups; One LifeWay Plaza; Nashville, TN 37234; or call toll free 800-458-2772.

With Explore the Bible, groups can expect to engage Scripture in its proper context and be better prepared to live it out in their own context. These book-by-book studies will help participants—

> grow in their love for Scripture;

> gain new knowledge about what the Bible teaches;

> develop biblical disciplines;

> internalize the Word in a way that transforms their lives.

 Connect

 @ExploreTheBible

 facebook.com/ExploreTheBible

 lifeway.com/ExploreTheBible

 ministrygrid.com/web/ExploreTheBible

❯ ABOUT THIS STUDY

WHERE DO YOU PUT YOUR FAITH?

Sometimes you don't know how things are going to work out. When the pressures of life are swirling all around you and a storm is raging within, where do you turn?

Having faith is more than hoping for the best or believing in yourself. Christian faith is trusting in someone greater than you and your circumstances. That person is Jesus.

The Bible's heroes of the faith were ordinary men and women who trusted an extraordinary God to lead them through seemingly impossible situations. That same faith is possible today.

Chapters 8–13 in the Book of Hebrews explore topics like living each day by faith, growing through hard times, the strength of covenant, and God's desire for life-changing community.

Explore the Bible: Hebrews, Chapters 8–13 will help you know and apply the encouraging and empowering truth of God's Word by organizing each session in the following way:

UNDERSTAND THE CONTEXT: This page explains the original context of each passage and begins relating the primary themes to your life today.

EXPLORE THE TEXT: This section walks you through the Scripture, providing helpful commentary and encouraging thoughtful interaction with God through His Word.

OBEY THE TEXT: This section helps you apply the truths you have explored. It is not enough to know what the Bible says—God's Word has the power to change your life.

LEADER GUIDE: This final section provides optional discussion starters and suggested questions to help anyone lead a group in reviewing each section of the personal study.

❯ GROUP COMMITMENT

As you begin this study, it is important that everyone agree to key group values. Clearly establishing the purpose of your time together will foster healthy expectations and help ease any uncertainties. The goal is to ensure that everyone has a positive experience leading to spiritual growth and true community. Initial each value as you discuss the following with your group.

❑ PRIORITY

Life is busy but we value this time with one another and with God's Word. We choose to make being together a priority.

❑ PARTICIPATION

We are a group. Everyone is encouraged to participate. No one dominates.

❑ RESPECT

Everyone is given the right to his or her own opinions. All questions are encouraged and respected.

❑ TRUST

Each person will humbly seek truth through time in prayer and in the Bible. We will trust God as the loving authority in our lives.

❑ CONFIDENTIALITY

Anything said in our meetings will never be repeated outside of the group without permission from everyone involved. This is vital in creating an environment of trust and openness.

❑ SUPPORT

Everyone can count on anyone in this group. Permission is given to call upon each other at any time, especially in times of crisis. The group will provide care for every member.

❑ ACCOUNTABILITY

We agree to let the members of our group hold us accountable to commitments we make in the loving ways we decide on. Questions are always welcome. Unsolicited advice, however, is not permitted.

_____   _____

I agree to all of the above.   Date

❯ GENERAL EDITOR

Dr. David Jeremiah serves as the senior pastor of Shadow Mountain Community Church in El Cajon, California. He is the founder and host of Turning Point, committed to providing Christians with sound Bible teaching relevant to today's changing times through radio and television, the Internet, live events, and resource materials and books. A best-selling author, Dr. Jeremiah has written more than 40 books, including *What Are You Afraid Of?* and its companion small-group study, and his study notes from over four decades have been compiled into *The Jeremiah Study Bible*.

Dr. Jeremiah's commitment to teaching the complete Word of God continues to make him a sought-after speaker and writer. His passion for reaching the lost and encouraging believers in their faith is demonstrated through his faithful communication of biblical truths.

A dedicated family man, Dr. Jeremiah and his wife, Donna, have 4 grown children and 11 grandchildren.

❯ CONTENTS

ONLY JESUS TRANSFORMS

Jesus established a new covenant based on God's good promises.

› UNDERSTAND THE CONTEXT

PREPARE FOR YOUR GROUP EXPERIENCE WITH THE FOLLOWING PAGES.

The writer of Hebrews spent a great deal of time and effort in the middle section of his book explaining the ministry of Jesus as the believer's Great High Priest.

In 8:1-6 the writer emphasized the main point of his effort. Jesus is now and forever seated at the right hand of the Father in heaven. He is in the true sanctuary of God, in the immediate presence of the Heavenly Father.

His ministry of advocating for believers is unending. There isn't a moment when Christ hits the pause button on interceding for His followers. For this reason, the new covenant in Christ is vastly better than any earthly priesthood and temple rituals. Those were never more than shadows of the salvation that comes through faith in Christ.

In 8:7-13 the writer took his readers back into the Old Testament and to a Scripture in which God promised that a new covenant would one day be established. Through the prophet Jeremiah, God had declared that the old covenant made through Moses would one day be replaced. It had proved to be inadequate, not because of anything lacking in God but because of the Israelites' constant disobedience.

The people needed more than rules to live by. They needed heart transformation. That transformation required a new and better covenant.

THE OLD COVENANT SPOKE OUTWARDLY TO THE INWARD MAN, BUT WHAT WAS NEEDED WAS SOMETHING THAT COULD SPEAK INWARDLY TO THE OUTWARD MAN. THE NEW COVENANT WAS GIVEN TO DO JUST THAT.

David Jeremiah

▶ HEBREWS 8:1-13

1 Now the main point of what is being said is this: We have this kind of high priest, who sat down at the right hand of the throne of the Majesty in the heavens,

2 a minister of the sanctuary and the true tabernacle that was set up by the Lord and not man.

3 For every high priest is appointed to offer gifts and sacrifices; therefore it was necessary for this priest also to have something to offer.

4 Now if He were on earth, He wouldn't be a priest, since there are those offering the gifts prescribed by the law.

5 These serve as a copy and shadow of the heavenly things, as Moses was warned when he was about to complete the tabernacle. For God said, Be careful that you make everything according to the pattern that was shown to you on the mountain.

6 But Jesus has now obtained a superior ministry, and to that degree He is the mediator of a better covenant, which has been legally enacted on better promises.

7 For if that first covenant had been faultless, there would have been no occasion for a second one.

8 But finding fault with His people, He says: Look, the days are coming, says the Lord, when I will make a new covenant with the house of Israel and with the house of Judah—

9 not like the covenant that I made with their ancestors on the day I took them by their hands to lead them out of the land of Egypt. I disregarded them, says the Lord, because they did not continue in My covenant.

10 But this is the covenant that I will make with the house of Israel after those days, says the Lord: I will put My laws into their minds and write them on their hearts. I will be their God, and they will be My people.

11 And each person will not teach his fellow citizen, and each his brother, saying, "Know the Lord," because they will all know Me, from the least to the greatest of them.

12 For I will be merciful to their wrongdoing, and I will never again remember their sins.

13 By saying, a new covenant, He has declared that the first is old. And what is old and aging is about to disappear.

Think About It

A covenant is an agreement governing a relationship. Highlight all the instances of the word covenant *in these verses. Take note of descriptive phrases that come before or after the word.*

Underline phrases that refer to the covenant God established in Jesus the Son.

> ABOUT THE BOOK OF HEBREWS

AUTHOR

The writer of Hebrews didn't identify himself, and Bible scholars haven't been able to determine who wrote it. Though we don't know the writer's identity, his spiritual maturity is evident within his writing. His writing reflected a devoted Christian leader who displayed passionate concern about believers considering retreat from Christianity.

AUDIENCE

Concerning the Christians to whom the Book of Hebrews was addressed, we can discern from the comparisons drawn in the text to key components of Judaism that they were believers, primarily from a Jewish background, who didn't have a clear understanding of who Jesus was. The persecution they were experiencing had caused them to reconsider their commitment to Christ, even being tempted to return to their traditional Jewish roots. Perhaps some of their friends and family members had been mistreated because of Christ. Or maybe they had experienced hard times themselves at the hands of adversaries of the gospel.

The strain of persecution apparently had been tempting them to consider an escape route. They still wanted to worship God, but they didn't want to live with the risk of more persecution. Details within the text suggest some were leaning toward returning to Judaism as an alternative. In their decision to embrace a safer way to serve God, they began distancing themselves from other Christians. The writer wanted them to work through any disillusionment by staying focused on Jesus and His superiority in their lives. Ultimately, they needed to be reminded of who He is.

PURPOSE

The writer of Hebrews made a passionate effort to persuade Christ-followers to maintain their faith in Jesus. He urged them to affirm the superiority of Christ above everything and everyone they had read about in the Old Testament. Then he encouraged them to consider God's perspective in their decision to possibly walk away from faith in Christ. Through God's eyes, they would surely understand why He would hold them accountable for misguided acts of disobedience and rebellion Finally, he challenged them to hold fast to the gospel, no matter the circumstances.

❯ EXPLORE THE TEXT

THE NEW COVENANT NEEDED *(Read Hebrews 8:1-6.)*

In these verses, the writer of Hebrews leads us to a critical point about Jesus that he wants us to grasp. Christ is the believer's High Priest, and He's altogether unique. He's the only One who is qualified to enter the true sanctuary of God in heaven on behalf of sinful humanity. To sit down at the right hand of God's throne means to keep dwelling there. In other words, Jesus has presence and authority with the Father in heaven.

In heaven, Jesus carries out the ongoing ministry as the believer's Great High Priest. The writer of Hebrews paints a picture of the distinct kind of sanctuary in heaven where Jesus dwells. For God's people in the days of the Old Testament, the sanctuary was the holy of holies in the tabernacle. The high priest would enter the holy of holies once each year on the Day of Atonement. For Christians, the heavenly sanctuary is the true and eternal dwelling of God.

What does the picture of Jesus' being seated at the Father's right hand say to you about Jesus' identity?

The writer of Hebrews goes on to describe the work Jesus carries out in the heavenly sanctuary. His description is set against the backdrop of the role of the Israelite high priest in Old Testament times. The

Israelite high priest offered sacrifices to God on behalf of His people. Jesus also offered a sacrifice for the sins of the people, but His sacrifice on the cross was once and for all. With that sacrifice Jesus alone qualified to be our High Priest in heaven. Yet He wouldn't have qualified to be a priest at the temple in Jerusalem. Jesus was of the tribe of Judah, not the tribe of Levi.

How would you describe the sacrifice that Jesus made on your behalf?

**Key Doctrine:
The New Covenant**
The new covenant is superior to the old covenant because it replaces external commandments with internal enablement, the ability to obey God's commands from the heart.

The tabernacle in the Old Testament and the priests who ministered in it were a mere copy and shadow of what God had established in heaven. The heavenly tabernacle was the true, perfect, and authentic sanctuary. God gave Moses a blueprint of that sanctuary while the Israelites were at Mount Sinai. God instructed Moses to carefully use the blueprint of the heavenly tabernacle as a pattern (see Ex. 25:40).

Just as God's tabernacle in heaven is the original, even so the matchless ministry of Jesus as our Great High Priest is the fulfillment of that which earthly high priests could only foreshadow. Jesus alone is qualified to be the perfect Mediator between God and His people. In Christ, the old covenant has been replaced by a new and better covenant. Christ is the guarantee of better promises.

How is salvation by faith in Jesus based on a better promise than a person's earning salvation by doing good works?

THE NEW COVENANT PROMISED

(Read Hebrews 8:7-9.)

In Christ, God established His new covenant. When God established the covenant with His people on Mount Sinai in Old Testament times, He revealed the law by which they were to live. If that covenant had been sufficient for our salvation from sin, then there would've been no need for Jesus to come and establish a new one. The first covenant revealed what was right and what was wrong in God's eyes, but it had no power to break the curse of sin or to transform the hearts of sinners. To be sure, mankind needed God's rules to live by, because without them we have always idolized our own thoughts and have been slaves to our fleshly desires (see Rom. 1:28-32). However, we needed more than a knowledge of God's law; we needed our hearts and minds to be transformed so that we could truly love God and desire His ways. We needed the power of sin to be broken.

The first readers of the Book of Hebrews knew the old covenant well. To drift from their confession of Christ back to the traditions of Judaism was to return to a covenant that was never able to save them from sin. The problem was not in something God did or didn't do in the first covenant. The problem was in the people's inability and unwillingness to obey the covenant. Through the Old Testament prophet Jeremiah, therefore, God declared that a new covenant would be given in the future (see Jer. 31:31-34).

What does God's promise of a new covenant teach about His love for all of humanity?

While the old covenant had to do with God's establishing a holy nation of people whom He rescued from slavery in Egypt, the new covenant would have a deeper purpose and a better promise.

THE NEW COVENANT DESCRIBED

(Read Hebrews 8:10-13.)

Looking ahead to those days when Christ would come, God proclaimed that the new covenant would be established with Israel. This new covenant would be characterized by God's gift of a new heart.

Through God's new covenant, His people no longer have His law written on tablets of stone. That's the way God's law was presented to the Israelites at Mount Sinai. In the new covenant, God would etch His law into their minds and write it on their hearts (see Phil. 2:13). Having been changed on the inside, the people would serve Him out of gratitude instead of duty.

How has God changed you from the inside out?
What difference has it made on the outside?

A most precious feature of the new covenant is God's willingness to be merciful toward sinners. In Christ, God does not give us the condemnation we deserve. Instead, He offers forgiveness. He takes away believers' guilt, frees them from sin's curse, and gives them new life. Because of His mercy shown in Christ's atoning death, the sins of His people will never be remembered again.

The writer of Hebrews concluded his quotation of Scripture by clarifying its meaning for his readers. If they were considering a return to their former life in Judaism, they needed to realize that the presence of a new covenant meant the old one was ready to pass away.

How has God's mercy influenced your walk with Christ?

What does God's promise of forgiveness say about His love for you?

Bible Skill: Observe when and for what purpose a New Testament passage includes an Old Testament quotation.

Identify the Old Testament passage quoted by the writer of Hebrews in Hebrews 8:8:b-12. Read the quoted passage in its Old Testament context. Then ask:

Why did the New Testament writer use the quoted passage? What factors are different in the old and new contexts? What factors are the same or similar? How does the quoted passage help you better understand Jesus and the gospel?

❯ OBEY THE TEXT

We are unable to keep God's law on our own. Only through faith in Christ can we be set free from sin to live a life that demonstrates righteousness.

Examine your prayer life, looking for attitudes and patterns that do not reflect a new heart. Identify ways you can reword those prayers in light of the new covenant.

What insights from this passage could you share with a friend who is trying to change his or her life apart from Christ? What do you need to let Jesus change in your life by trusting in Him and not in yourself?

What needs to change in your Bible study group so that the group reflects the attitudes and characteristics presented in this passage? What action do you need to take as a part of that group to make the needed changes?

MEMORIZE

"I will be merciful to their wrongdoing, and I will never again remember their sins" (Hebrews 8:12).

Use the space provided to make observations and record prayer requests during the group experience for this session.

MY THOUGHTS

Record insights and questions from the group experience.

_____
_____
_____
_____
_____
_____

MY RESPONSE

Note specific ways you will put into practice the truth explored this week.

_____
_____
_____
_____
_____
_____

MY PRAYERS

List specific prayer needs and answers to remember this week.

_____
_____
_____
_____
_____
_____

THE PERFECT OFFERING

Christ's atoning sacrifice established a new covenant of eternal redemption.

⟩ UNDERSTAND THE CONTEXT

PREPARE FOR YOUR GROUP EXPERIENCE WITH THE FOLLOWING PAGES.

The Old Testament tabernacle and the annual atonement sacrifice offered there served as starting points for the writer of Hebrews to explain the new covenant centered in Jesus Christ and His once-for-all sacrifice. Mentioning the tabernacle was helpful because it was a respected place of worship in Israelite history. For that reason, the readers of Hebrews, with their background in Judaism, were intimately familiar with it.

The writer showed that the animal sacrifices offered at the tabernacle never had the power in themselves to break sin's curse or transform the human heart. Only the precious blood of Christ could make the removal of our sin possible (9:1-15).

Then the writer drew upon the analogy of a last will and testament to show that Christ had to die in order for believers to receive the inheritance God promised them. The writer followed the same line of reasoning when he insisted that blood had to be shed in order for sins to be forgiven. That's why only the shed blood of Jesus can break sin's curse and restore the sinner to a right relationship with God. Christ's sacrifice has removed believers' sin-debt once and for all (9:16-28).

Pointing to the tabernacle once more, the writer of Hebrews warned again that animal sacrifices can never take away our sins. Christ's death on the cross was the only sufficient sacrifice. God's righteousness demanded a qualified sacrifice for sin, but animal sacrifices were unable to provide it. However, Christ's perfect sacrifice on the cross accomplished God's will by making atonement for our sin. The writer went on to validate his assertion about Jesus with Scripture passages that clearly affirm God's way of forgiveness (10:1-18).

> ONLY BY BEING BOTH DEITY AND HUMANITY COULD JESUS CHRIST BRIDGE THE GAP BETWEEN WHERE WE ARE AND WHERE GOD IS. WITHOUT JESUS CHRIST, THERE IS NO HOPE OF ANY OF US EVER HAVING A RELATIONSHIP WITH THE HOLY GOD.
> *David Jeremiah*

11 But the Messiah has appeared, **high priest** of the good things that have come. In the greater and more perfect tabernacle not made with hands (that is, not of this creation),

12 He entered the most holy place once for all, not by the blood of goats and calves, but by His own blood, having obtained eternal redemption.

13 For if the blood of goats and bulls and the ashes of a young cow, sprinkling those who are defiled, sanctify for the purification of the flesh,

14 how much more will the blood of the **Messiah**, who through the **eternal Spirit** offered Himself without blemish to God, cleanse our consciences from dead works to serve the living God?

15 Therefore, He is the **mediator** of a new covenant, so that those who are called might receive the promise of the eternal inheritance, because a death has taken place for redemption from the transgressions committed under the first covenant.

Think About It

Highlight all the titles (look for nouns) in these verses that identify Jesus. What do these titles say to you about Jesus' saving work?

Take note of words and phrases that point to the superiority of Jesus' saving work over the old (first) covenant.

EXPLORE THE TEXT

CHRIST'S ENTRY *(Read Hebrews 9:11-12.)*

The heavenly sanctuary, or tabernacle, was greater and more perfect than the earthly representation. The earthly tabernacle was only a shadow of God's sanctuary in heaven. To be sure, it gave a true picture of God's dwelling. But like a blueprint is to an actual building, the earthly tabernacle could only hint at the glorious reality of the heavenly one.

Since the tabernacle was where the Israelites of Old Testament times gathered to meet with God, it shaped the religious life of the nation. Its revered place in Israel's history helped the writer of Hebrews to drive home the truth about Jesus. The picture of the tabernacle could help believers grasp more completely everything Jesus had done to provide the way of salvation.

The atoning sacrifice of Christ through His death on the cross made salvation possible. Having been forgiven and made right with God, they entered a new covenant relationship with Him. His laws were planted in their hearts, blossoming into lifestyles that reflected His righteousness in them. Furthermore, they could count on Christ's ongoing presence and power when they faced tough times, and they could look forward to being in heaven with their Lord and Savior when they died.

In the Old Testament tabernacle, the high priest entered the holy of holies—where the ark of the covenant rested—once each year on the Day of Atonement. Reflecting on that picture, the readers of Hebrews could better grasp the image of Jesus entering the most holy place in the heavenly tabernacle. However, Jesus didn't have to leave and re-enter the heavenly holy of holies each year. His death on the cross uniquely qualified Him to enter the most holy place in the heavenly tabernacle once and for all.

As Jesus made the final and complete entry into the holy of holies in heaven, He brought with Him a priceless offering. In Old Testament times, the high priest of the day brought the blood of animal sacrifices into the most holy place for making the atoning offering. Jesus didn't present the blood of sacrificed animals as an offering to God. Instead, He presented His own shed blood. With His matchless offering, Jesus purchased believers' salvation. He set us free by paying the price of atonement that we couldn't pay and for which animal sacrifices could not qualify.

How does your awareness of what Jesus has done impact how you worship?

CHRIST'S SUPERIOR SACRIFICE *(Read Hebrews 9:13-14.)*

The first ceremony involved the blood of goats and bulls. On the Day of Atonement, the Israelite high priest sacrificed these two animals and sprinkled their blood on the mercy seat in the holy of holies (see Lev. 16:11-17). The second ceremony occurred when needed and involved a young cow. The high priest sacrificed a red heifer and burned it to ashes on the altar. The ashes would be collected and sprinkled on the water that was used to cleanse a person who had been defiled by touching a dead body (see Num. 19:1-10).

God's people who participated in worship practices that involved these elements would be purified, but only on the outside. That is, the blood and ashes served to cleanse the flesh. However, those sacrifices could not make a person pure on the inside.

In what ways have you seen people try to make themselves pure before God?

What are the shortcomings of these efforts?

The blood of Jesus alone cleanses us on the inside. The Son of God took on human flesh and lived among us for the purpose of offering Himself as a sacrifice in our place. By dying on the cross, He paid our sin-debt so that we might be set free from the curse of sin. With His blood, He cleanses us on the inside and makes us spiritually pure before God.

Jesus was the perfect sacrifice because He was without sin. God commanded His people to bring only unblemished red heifers to the altar as sacrifices (see Num. 19:2). In keeping with God's command, Jesus is completely flawless inside and outside. None of the defects caused by sin can be found in Him. Because He's perfectly sinless, He stands alone as the ultimate and final sacrifice for our sins.

The phrase "through the eternal Spirit" can refer either to the Holy Spirit's involvement in Jesus' offering Himself as a sacrifice to the Father—and thus a reference to the Trinity working in unity to bring about salvation—or to the spiritual nature of Jesus' atoning sacrifice. In either view the conclusion is that Christ presented Himself to God as the perfect offering.

**Key Doctrine:
Bought by His Blood**

Salvation involves the redemption of the whole person, and is offered freely to all who accept Jesus Christ as Lord and Savior, who by His own blood obtained eternal redemption for the believer.

In what ways do you devote yourself to serving God from a pure conscience?

How is a Christian's motive for service different from the motives of non-Christians?

CHRIST'S MEDIATION *(Read Hebrews 9:15.)*

A mediator stands between two parties who need to arrive at an agreement, or covenant. By presenting His own blood to God as an atoning sacrifice, Jesus alone has the authority to bring us into a new relationship with a Holy God.

When two people make an agreement, they ratify it—put it into effect by some significant action. When a man and a woman enter into a marriage relationship, they signify it by exchanging vows and often by exchanging rings. Similarly, God has established a new covenant for sinners in the shed blood of Jesus Christ (see Luke 22:20). Through faith in Jesus, we become participants in the new covenant. God implants His Spirit and His Word in us in a way that transforms us spiritually. Such a remarkable covenant could only be possible because Jesus, the Great High Priest, presented His own blood as an offering to God so that we could be saved.

Because of the new covenant Jesus enacted by His atoning death, we receive an incredible surplus of rich blessings from God when we receive Christ as Savior. The writer of Hebrews describes these blessings as our eternal inheritance. Like a person who has written in a will what all family members will inherit, God has determined our inheritance.

We can be assured of receiving this wonderful inheritance, because we serve a God who always keeps His promises. Through the prophet Jeremiah, God promised that He would establish a new covenant (Jer. 31:31-34). He kept that promise when Jesus established the new covenant in His blood.

The new covenant has been made possible through Christ, our Mediator. When Christ gave His life on the cross for us, He overcame the enslaving power of sin and death. The old covenant with its animal sacrifices could never provide what God has freely given us in the new covenant in Christ.

How does the idea of Jesus being the perfect Mediator impact your understanding of Him?

Bible Skill: Connect Old Testament prophecy to New Testament fulfillment.

Read Jeremiah 31:31-34 and take note of the main features of the "new covenant" that the prophet foresaw. Then read Luke 22:20 and observe what Jesus said about the new covenant.

How does the fulfillment of prophecy support what the writer of Hebrews stated in Hebrews 9:15?

❯ OBEY THE TEXT

Followers of Christ find rest from the demands of legalism. Christ gives believers a clear conscience to serve Him with a pure heart.

In what ways does salvation in Christ help you move beyond moral failures?

Identify and evaluate ways your group can appropriately express gratitude for Christ's sacrifice into corporate worship services.

What motivates you to serve Christ? Identify acts of service you could do in the next week that could be done anonymously (no one knows but you and God) and put those into action. Record insights gained from the experience.

MEMORIZE

"He is the mediator of a new covenant, so that those who are called might receive the promise of the eternal inheritance, because a death has taken place for redemption from the transgressions committed under the first covenant" (Hebrews 9:15).

Use the space provided to make observations and record prayer requests during the group experience for this session.

MY THOUGHTS

Record insights and questions from the group experience.

_____

_____

_____

_____

_____

_____

MY RESPONSE

Note specific ways you will put into practice the truth explored this week.

_____

_____

_____

_____

_____

_____

MY PRAYERS

List specific prayer needs and answers to remember this week.

_____

_____

_____

_____

_____

_____

FAITH DEFINED

A relationship with God begins with faith in Jesus.

>> UNDERSTAND THE CONTEXT

PREPARE FOR YOUR GROUP EXPERIENCE WITH THE FOLLOWING PAGES.

The term *faith* is an important word in the Bible, appearing well over 200 times in the New Testament. The writer of Hebrews used the term more than 20 times just in chapter 11. When he used this word, he had in mind a Christian's complete trust in the Lord and firm reliance on Him alone.

Some level of persecution had brought on tough times for the first readers of Hebrews. The writer reminded them that they had endured hardships in the past. Their enduring faith would compel them to keep on standing firm in Christ as they faced difficult days in the present or future (10:38-39).

The writer then moved on in his letter to focus the attention of these troubled Christians on the value of trusting the Lord as they struggled through painful circumstances. First, he defined faith in terms that would show them what it meant to live by faith (11:1-3).

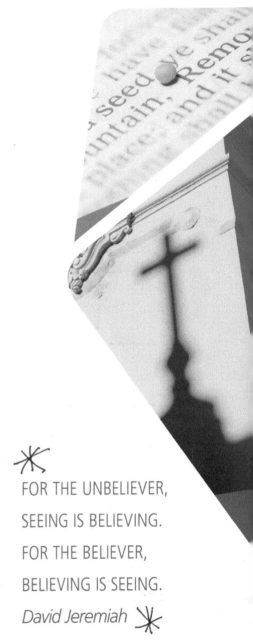

Next the writer gave some persuasive examples from Old Testament times of people who trusted God in the face of challenging ordeals. Drawing from the Old Testament Scriptures, he brought to mind three of his readers' Israelite ancestors: Abel, Enoch, and Noah (11:4-7).

FOR THE UNBELIEVER, SEEING IS BELIEVING. FOR THE BELIEVER, BELIEVING IS SEEING.
David Jeremiah

Then he recounted the faith of Abraham, Sarah, Isaac, and Joseph (11:8-22). From there, he reminded them that Moses and others trusted God as they guided His people to possess the promised land (11:23-31). Finally, the writer listed others whose faith in the Lord enabled them to experience victory. Faith in God strengthened His people to stand firm as they endured extreme hardships (11:32-38). He emphasized that Old Testament believers remained faithful even though they didn't live to see the new covenant enacted in Christ (11:39-40).

❯ HEBREWS 11:1-7

1 Now <u>faith</u> is the reality of what is hoped for, the proof of what is not seen.

2 For our ancestors won God's approval by it.

3 <u>By faith</u> we understand that the universe was created by God's command, so that what is seen has been made from things that are not visible.

4 <u>By faith</u> Abel offered to God a better sacrifice than Cain did. <u>By faith</u> he was approved as a righteous man, because God approved his gifts, and even though he is dead, he still speaks through his faith.

5 <u>By faith</u> Enoch was taken away so he did not experience death, and he was not to be found because God took him away. For prior to his removal he was approved, since he had pleased God.

6 Now <u>without faith</u> it is impossible to please God, for the one who draws near to Him must believe that He exists and rewards those who seek Him.

7 <u>By faith</u> Noah, after he was warned about what was not yet seen and motivated by godly fear, built an ark to deliver his family. <u>By faith</u> he condemned the world and became an heir of the righteousness that comes <u>by faith</u>.

they didn't have boats back then

> ## Think About It

Observe all the instances of the phrase "by faith" in these verses. What does this phrase emphasize to you? What other phrases containing the word faith appear in these verses?

Take note of the actions by which Abel, Enoch, and Noah demonstrated their faith in God. Highlight actions God took in response to each man's faith.

❯ EXPLORE THE TEXT

FAITH DESCRIBED *(Read Hebrews 11:1-3.)*

The first verse in Hebrews 11 seizes our attention. It casts our gaze on faith and encourages us to place our trust only in the Lord. Our complete trust in God makes us certain about what we hope for in Him. Also, it makes us absolutely sure about the existence of what God has promised even though we cannot see it yet.

What might anxiety about the future say about a person's trust in God? In your understanding, what is the difference between faith and hope?

> With faith we don't have highs + lows. We need to focus on God not our worries.
>
> *knowledge.*
> faith = a knowing trust in God
>
> *feeling*
> hope = wishing trust in man

Faith in the Lord makes a huge difference in the way mature followers of Christ face adversity. That's what the writer of Hebrews wanted his first readers to grasp. Their faith in God needed to be made evident in the way they lived, just as it did in the lives of God's faithful people in Old Testament times.

Both the writer and the first Christians who read his epistle had great respect for the spiritual leaders of Old Testament Israel. They served in effect as role models of genuine faith in God. Their faith served as the foundation for God's approval of their lives. For them, being right with God didn't result from what they did but from the One they believed in. Their faith bore witness to the reality that they belonged to the Lord God and to Him alone.

Who might be observing you at this time as a role model of trusting in God in the face of uncertainties?

> Kids
> less mature Christians

The writer directs us to consider God's creation, an amazing wonder that we can see all around us. The universe displays a fundamental connection between God and His people. God created the universe with His command, yet no human being was there to see Him while He did it.

Likewise, no human was around to look over God's shoulder and to give a report when He formed the world and made all that inhabits it. But we don't actually need a human eyewitness to creation who can testify that God created everything we see. The way that we know God created all that exists is by revelation: He tells us in His Word that He did.

In the same way, our trust in God enables us to settle all the mysteries about how He brought the universe into existence. Our faith in Him prompts us to rest in the assurance that when He created time and space, He made the visible out of the invisible. Believing in Him enables us to praise Him for creating our incredible world out of absolutely nothing except the exquisite, powerful thoughts in His infinite mind.

When was the last time you observed the connection between the Creator and His creation? What were you observing? How did you respond to the observation?

His creation is very diverse, yet ordered.
Echo. Nature.
Creation knows who its Creator is!

FAITH DEMONSTRATED
(Read Hebrews 11:4-7.)

The writer introduced a heroes' list, a roll call of faith, that described Old Testament believers who lived by faith even before the Author and Finisher of faith appeared on the scene. The writer began with Abel, a son of the first human couple, Adam and Eve. Abel demonstrated genuine faith in God by presenting to the Lord a proper sacrifice (see Gen. 4:3-5). Abel's sacrifice stood in stark contrast to an offering given by his brother, Cain. The entire episode, which includes Cain's vengeful murder of Abel, shows that God approves the kind of faithful obedience represented in offering a proper sacrifice.

Equally noteworthy for the writer of Hebrews was the fact that God declared Abel to be a righteous man (see Heb. 11:4). Abel was right with God, but his righteousness, or right standing, didn't result from his own ability to give a better offering than Cain. It resulted from his complete faith in God. Abel died, but the story about him and his faith in the Lord continued to live on across the centuries.

What do your offerings reveal about your faith in God?

They reflect your depth of faith.

The next hero of faith on the writer's list was Enoch. Genesis 5:21-24 provides us with a brief account of Enoch's walk of faith with God. It is contained in a genealogy of Seth, the son of Adam and Eve who was born after Abel was murdered (see Gen. 5:3). Enoch's faith was made evident in that God simply took him to heaven without death.

The reference to Enoch gave the writer of Hebrews an opening to emphasize that it is by trusting completely in God that we please Him. In fact, without faith we cannot please Him. This is a crucial life principle

> **Key Doctrine: Faith**
>
> Repentance and faith are inseparable experiences of grace. Faith is the acceptance of Jesus Christ and commitment of the entire person to Him as Lord and Savior.

for growing believers. The principle offers Christians then and now the way forward as we give attention to nurturing a lifestyle of trust in God.

When we receive His gift of salvation by faith, we begin a lifelong journey of trust and obedience. Christ leads; we follow. We keep our eyes on Him even as the uncertainties and challenges of life swirl around us. Every step in our walk with the Lord is a step of faith. And our faith pleases Him.

The writer's next Old Testament example of faith was Noah. The account of Noah's life can be found in Genesis 5:28–9:29. Noah was Enoch's great-grandson. Like Enoch, Noah walked in faith with God. He placed his trust completely in the Lord, and he lived in obedience to God's ways. During Noah's lifetime, the Lord warned this man of faith that He was about to judge the earth because of humanity's great wickedness. This judgment would come as a worldwide flood. The Lord directed Noah to build a massive ark, fill it according to His instructions, and wait for the flood that would come in due time.

When God revealed that He would destroy the earth because of the wickedness and corruption among the people, Noah took Him seriously. He walked faithfully with the Lord and obeyed His directions without fail. For 120 years, people lived as though God didn't exist. But Noah believed that God would do what He promised. In the face of an unbelieving world, Noah stood faithful and showed that he trusted in the Lord. Because of his faithfulness and obedience, Noah pleased the Lord.

Faith in Jesus

Similar to Noah, we may have to endure times of hardship and opposition before we see with our eyes what our faith in God leads us to embrace. We please God by living in faith, putting our lives and futures completely in His hands. Our faith in Him will be demonstrated by the actions we take as we serve Him.

How are faith in God and obedience to His ways related?

When we are obedient our faith ↑

Have to have faith to be
          obedient

**Bible Skill:
Memorize a verse
and apply it to a
real life situation.**

Memorize
Hebrews 11:6 in
your preferred Bible
translation. Then
write the verse in your
own words. Finally,
write a couple of
sentences here or in
a journal, stating how
the verse can help
you today to make a
tough decision or face
a difficult situation.

Can you have one without the other? Explain.

Sometimes. Process. Both grow.
Jump in. Level of faith.

❯ OBEY THE TEXT

Real faith is trusting God with all our lives, including our future. Real faith leads to actions that demonstrate trust in God and His promises. God is pleased when we act upon our faith in Him.

What actions can you take to develop a faith like Abel, Enoch, or Noah?

Upon what one promise of God is He calling you to take action? What is your plan of action?

What action(s) can you take to stretch and grow your faith in God? How can your Bible study group help one another stretch and grow in their faith in God?

MEMORIZE

"Without faith it is impossible to please God, for the one who draws near to Him must believe that He exists and rewards those who seek Him" (Hebrews 11:6).

Use the space provided to make observations and record prayer requests during the group experience for this session.

MY THOUGHTS

Record insights and questions from the group experience.

_____

_____

_____

_____

_____

_____

MY RESPONSE

Note specific ways you will put into practice the truth explored this week.

_____

_____

_____

_____

_____

_____

MY PRAYERS

List specific prayer needs and answers to remember this week.

Cynthia - mother of coworker going blind
Barry - Kerri's family/house process
Mom → biopsy negative
Dave → radiation process
Marriages, Dan

THE DISCIPLINE OF SUFFERING

Christ's perfect sacrifice calls for His followers to remain faithful regardless.

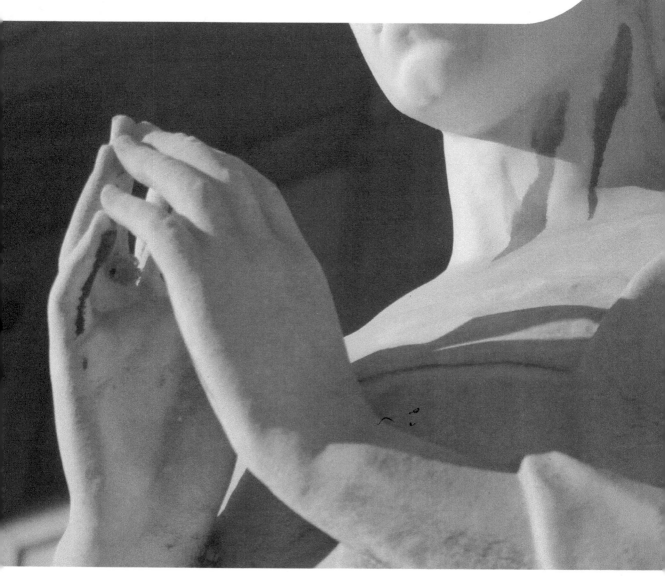

› UNDERSTAND THE CONTEXT

PREPARE FOR YOUR GROUP EXPERIENCE WITH THE FOLLOWING PAGES.

As we've seen throughout Hebrews, the writer combined explanation and exhortation to persuade his Christian brothers and sisters to cling to Jesus and grow in their faith. God's Son is the final and ultimate Word from God; therefore, salvation in Him must not be neglected (2:4). Jesus is our Great High Priest; so then, we must stop acting like spiritual babies and go on to a mature faith in Him *going over it again + again* (6:1). Jesus established the new covenant in His shed blood on the cross; therefore, we can draw near to Him in faith, holding to Him in all situations as our true hope (10:22-23), and encouraging one another in the fellowship of the church (10:24-25).

Hebrews 11 is a roll call of Old Testament individuals whose lives defined literally what it means to live by faith. These were God's people who lived under the old covenant, yet they showed through their actions that they believed God one day was going to do something new (11:10,19,26). They looked forward to the fulfillment of God's promise, though they didn't see it in their lifetimes (11:39-40).

The readers of Hebrews, however, lived in the age of gospel fulfillment. Jesus had come, given His life on the cross, and been raised from the dead to enter God's heavenly sanctuary once and for all. These readers professed faith in Christ, and they needed to realize they were surrounded by a cloud of witnesses, whose lives urged them on in the race of faith (12:1-3).

With their focus on Jesus, the readers of Hebrews could run the race and finish it well. They needed to embrace God's perspective on their suffering. God would use their hardships and persecution as training, or discipline. In doing so, God was treating them as His children, not as outcasts. He is a loving Father who deeply wants His children to grow strong in their faith (12:4-13).

> LIFE IS ABOUT DOING HARD THINGS THAT YOU DON'T WANT TO DO BECAUSE YOU BELIEVE THE RESULT OF DOING THOSE HARD THINGS IS GOING TO CREATE GREAT JOY AND GREAT GOOD— NOT ONLY FOR YOU AND FOR OTHERS, BUT MOST OF ALL FOR THE GLORY OF THE LORD JESUS CHRIST.
>
> *David Jeremiah*

➤ HEBREWS 12:1-7

1 Therefore, since we also have such a large cloud of witnesses surrounding us, let us lay aside every weight and the sin that so easily ensnares us. Let us run with endurance the race that lies before us,

2 keeping our eyes on Jesus, the source and perfecter of our faith, who for the joy that lay before Him endured a cross and despised the shame and has sat down at the right hand of God's throne.

3 For consider Him who endured such hostility from sinners against Himself, so that you won't grow weary and lose heart.

4 In struggling against sin, you have not yet resisted to the point of shedding your blood.

5 And you have forgotten the exhortation that addresses you as sons: My son, do not take the Lord's discipline lightly or faint when you are reproved by Him,

reprimands

6 for the Lord disciplines the one He loves and punishes every son He receives.

7 Endure suffering as discipline: God is dealing with you as sons. For what son is there that a father does not discipline?

running
blaming
asking why

Psalm 91

Think About It

Observe the "let us" phrases in verse 1. Take note of what the writer urged his readers to join him in doing.

Highlight in verses 5-7 all terms that refer to God's correction of His people. What are ways that people might respond to correction?

❯ EXPLORE THE TEXT

ENDURING (Read Hebrews 12:1-3.)

Every generation of believers is surrounded by a cloud of witnesses. One way of understanding this imagery is to picture a stadium packed with cheering fans. The fans are past believers, finishers, who look on and root for the present generation of Christians as they run the race of faith. Another way to understand the picture in verse 1, however, is to imagine the readers of Hebrews looking at the host of finishers who've gone before them.

Whose story of faith inspires you to keep on trusting Jesus?

family members
friends
biblical people

In either understanding, the point was for the readers (and us) to be encouraged in their faith. They were running a long-distance race, not a sprint. They needed to keep going, to endure. To help us endure and finish well in our faith, we must lay aside any habit, attitude, or thought that drains our trust in Christ. It is the energizing work of the Holy Spirit that helps us lay aside these weights (see Phil. 2:13).

Believers also falter by falling into sin. Unconfessed sins are like lead weights chained to a runner's ankles. Proverbs 28:13 teaches that the one who tries to conceal sin will not prosper, but the one who repents and confesses will receive mercy. First John 1:9 teaches also that if we confess our sins, God will forgive and cleanse us from all unrighteousness. Mature Christians are to help a stumbling believer seek restoration in Christ (see Gal. 6:1).

We can also endure by looking to Jesus as the Champion of champions when it comes to living by faith. Even the spiritual heroes whose portraits hang in the Faith Hall of Fame had times of weakness and distraction. But not Jesus. In His time on earth, Jesus exemplified the life of faith from start to finish. He is faith's pioneer and perfecter.

When runners get distracted during a race, they can lose focus. They get off track or forget their game plan for reaching the finish line. Similarly, Christians who get distracted in life—who fail to keep their focus on God's plan for them—often get off track spiritually.

For this reason, Jesus deserves our complete attention. He is the original Author of our faith. Moreover, He perfected faith. He completed it. He lived by faith in the Heavenly Father from start to finish. Therefore, we as Christ's followers gain strength for endurance as we keep our eyes fixed on Him.

What situations might cause you to become spiritually distracted? How can you avoid getting off track?

Crowd
prosperity
offense
justifying

positive assoc
fellowship
stay in the word

Jesus endured unthinkable suffering on the cross, not because of any wrongdoing by Him, but as the atoning sacrifice for our sins. Providing the way of salvation for us was the prize, the joy, that was His focus when He poured out His heart in the garden; when He stood accused and condemned by religious leaders; when mallet blows drove spikes through His hands and feet, pinning Him to the cross; and when with a final breath He cried out, "It is finished!" (John 19:30).

The faith by which Jesus laid down His life on our behalf was a victorious faith. He arose from the dead! He utterly defeated sin and death. And now, as the Great High Priest, He is seated forever at the right hand of God's throne. His victory guarantees the victory of all who run the race of life by faith in Him.

The writer of Hebrews urged his readers to think seriously and carefully about Jesus and what He endured for their sake. Were they experiencing hostility, opposition, or hardships because of their confession of Christ? Were they growing weary and fearful? If they focused on Jesus, they would know that He understood the cost of discipleship more than they ever could. They would also realize that all power in heaven and on earth belongs to Him, and that He strengthens His followers so they can endure any hardship or persecution.

Key Doctrine: The Father Who Cares

God as Father reigns with providential care over His universe, His creatures, and the flow of the stream of human history according to the purposes of His grace.

How would you describe what it takes to finish well in life?

perseverance
discipline
athletes → nourishment, focus, training
growth share our faith
surround yourselves w/ the people athletes do i.e. coaches, fellow athletes, etc.

DISCIPLINED (Read Hebrews 12:4-7.)

Olympic athletes don't wait until the games to start training. Most of them have trained since childhood, practicing hours a day every day—sweating, exercising, studying, focusing, eating right—just for the moment they compete on the world stage at the Olympics.

Staying focused on training requires discipline. Likewise, discipline is required in our training as champions of Christ. The writer of Hebrews addressed this requirement with his readers. Some of them were faltering in their faith and struggling against sin, however none of the readers had yet suffered to the point of martyrdom. If martyrdom occurred in the future, they were to remember that Jesus endured the cross, and He holds the crown of life (see Rev. 2:10).

What kinds of training do Christ followers need?

See previous page

How does discipline fit in?

everywhere + in everything

The writer turned once again to the Old Testament Scriptures to exhort his readers. They were suffering hardships, but what was their attitude about their suffering? Were they losing heart or growing bitter against God? Did they understand the positive value of seeing their situation as divine discipline? The writer used Proverbs 3:11-12 to show that God's discipline—even His corrective chastening— was evidence that they were God's children.

The stated purpose of Proverbs is to provide God's people with training in righteousness (see Prov. 1:3; 2 Tim. 3:16-17). In Proverbs 3:11-12, Solomon taught his son the reason to value God's corrective discipline. The writer of Hebrews knew that his readers also needed to hear that message.

God's corrective discipline has a positive purpose. It is meant to help us stay on track and strengthen us, so that we will love and trust Him more. God uses it to build our spiritual endurance.

How has God been nurturing your faith in Him?

fellowship
speaking to me
how He's worked thru others

What role has adversity played in His nurturing?

deployment
Cancer
valley vs. mountain

Children have a tendency to be excellent observers but poor interpreters of what's going on around them. God's children often suffer from a similar tendency. If we're not careful, we can allow ourselves to believe that God has allowed turmoil to overwhelm us because He's spiteful or simply doesn't care what happens to us.

But God isn't spiteful; He loves us. He prepares us through discipline so that we can endure and overcome adversity, not just simply escape it. His discipline underscores the depth of His love for us and the authenticity of our faith in Him.

How does trust in God and His discipline impact your view of difficult situations?

He uses all for good.
Choices vs. God

Bible Skill:
Identify the imagery in a verse or passage and discover what it communicates.

List words and phrases in Hebrews 12:1-2 that describe an endurance race. *perseverance*
endurance

What does each word and phrase communicate to you about following Christ?

How is the imagery of endurance in a race like and unlike the endurance of God's correction mentioned in 12:7?

Growth in Character

❯ OBEY THE TEXT

Christians are called to live out their faith consistently throughout their lifetimes, striving to finish well. Running the race of faith may include physical suffering for the sake of Christ. The believer can find strength in Christ to endure adversity and to be strengthened by discipline.

On a scale of 1 to 10, with 1 being poor and 10 being excellent, how would you rate your faith in God? What entanglements do you need to remove so that you can finish strong? What step can you take this week to remove those entanglements?

How is God using a difficulty to shape you and grow your trust in Him? How can you use what you are learning to help another person in your Bible study group?

Search the Internet, looking for stories of Christians being persecuted for their faith. Identify ways you can encourage them and learn from them. How can your Bible study group help you encourage and learn from persecuted believers?

MEMORIZE ❯

"The Lord disciplines the one He loves, and punishes every son He receives" (Hebrews 12:6).

Use the space provided to make observations and record prayer requests during the group experience for this session.

MY THOUGHTS

Record insights and questions from the group experience.

_____
_____
_____
_____
_____
_____

MY RESPONSE

Note specific ways you will put into practice the truth explored this week.

_____
_____
_____
_____
_____
_____

MY PRAYERS

List specific prayer needs and answers to remember this week.

Cynthia – Tony's legs
Mom – biopsy
Krista + family

A NEW KIND OF COMMUNITY

Because of the blood of Jesus, believers can have joyful fellowship with one another and with God.

❯ UNDERSTAND THE CONTEXT

PREPARE FOR YOUR GROUP EXPERIENCE WITH THE FOLLOWING PAGES.

The believers who first received this epistle were challenged to live according to God's standard of behavior. God intended for them to live in peace with one another and with pure hearts before Him. Such a critical mandate required them to keep their relationships free from bitterness. They also needed to encourage one another to avoid an ungodly lifestyle characterized by immorality.

In Old Testament times, Esau was an example of one who gave himself to self-indulgent behavior, and he paid a high price for his sinfulness (12:14-17).

Along with nurturing relationships that honor the Lord, readers were also urged to embrace the new covenant. In order to help them live in the new covenant and not revert to the old, the writer compared Mount Sinai with Mount Zion. At Mount Sinai, God's people received the law and lived it out in a setting marked by terrifying fear. At Mount Zion, however, the foundation of a believer's relationship with God was the good news of Jesus Christ. In Christ, believers live in joyful fellowship with God and one another. The new covenant established a new community of God's people (12:18-24).

In the new covenant community, devotion to Christ is the highest priority for believers. Instead of giving themselves to kingdoms that could be shaken, they would do well to keep in mind that they belonged to God's kingdom. Therefore, Christians needed to take seriously the aim of godly lifestyles. Otherwise, they would face God's discipline. They could count on God to hold them accountable if they gave themselves to ungodly behavior (12:25-29).

MOUNT SINAI GAVE THE LAW THAT ONLY THE CROSS COULD SATISFY.
David Jeremiah

❯ HEBREWS 12:18-24

18 For you have not come to what could be touched, to a blazing fire, to darkness, gloom, and storm,

19 to the blast of a trumpet, and the sound of words. (Those who heard it begged that not another word be spoken to them,

20 for they could not bear what was commanded: And if even an animal touches the mountain, it must be stoned!

21 The appearance was so terrifying that Moses said, I am terrified and trembling.)

22 Instead, you have come to Mount Zion, to the city of the living God (the heavenly Jerusalem), to myriads of angels in festive gathering,

23 to the assembly of the firstborn whose names have been written in heaven, to God who is the Judge of all, to the spirits of righteous people made perfect,

24 to Jesus (mediator of a new covenant), and to the sprinkled blood, which says better things than the blood of Abel.

Think About It

Take note of the sights and sounds mentioned in verses 18-21. What response did they evoke from people?

Highlight the sights in verses 22-24 associated with Mount Zion. What response do you have in thinking about those sights?

❯ EXPLORE THE TEXT

FROM A TERRIFYING ENCOUNTER
(Read Hebrews 12:18-21.)

In calling for his readers to live holy lives, the writer recalled the sights and sounds of the old covenant's launch. God's awesome presence on the mountain was attested by a chilling darkness, lightning, thick smoke, blazing fire, and the deafening, continuous sound of a blaring trumpet (see Ex. 19:16-19). God spoke to Moses with thunderous words, and delivered to Moses the Commandments governing the people's relationship with Him and with one another (see Ex. 19:19; 20:1-17).

The Israelites were petrified! They begged for Moses to be a go-between. They didn't want to hear another word from God directly, for fear of dying (see Ex. 20:18-19). The encounter left them with an indelible impression of fear and dread that settled deeply within them.

What experiences have you had that deeply impressed you regarding God's holiness, power, revelation of truth?

The writer of Hebrews recalled this scene to remind his Christian friends that the new covenant was ratified in a different way than that of the old covenant. For believers to drift away from Christ and to consider a return to Judaism was unthinkable. They would be returning to the old covenant demands of the law, which evoked the fear of death rather than gave the hope of forgiveness and new life.

Even though the Israelites could hear the sound of God's voice coming from the mountain, they couldn't approach the mountain to get close to Him. The mountain had been declared off limits to them. If they disobeyed Him and tried to make their way up the mountain with Moses, they were to be stoned.

According to God's command, any animal or individual who dared to approach Him on Mount Sinai would be put to death (see Ex. 19:12). For the Lord, the issue of coming into His presence was serious business. The penalty He imposed on anyone who disobeyed His command no doubt compounded the terrifying fear that marked the encounter His people had with Him.

When does the awareness of God's presence make you afraid? When are you comforted by that awareness?

God's people weren't alone in their fear as they stood at the foot of Mount Sinai. Their leader, Moses, was also terrified. The people watched Moses as he made his way up the mountain to talk with God about the covenant. They could tell by Moses' appearance that being in the presence of God frightened him.

In Deuteronomy 9:19, four decades after the actual event, Moses addressed the new generation of Israelites who would enter and take possession of the promised land. He recalled the fear that gripped him when he came down from the mountain with God's law written on the stone tablets. That's when he saw that the people of Israel had erected a golden calf to worship. The spectacle made Moses tremble in fear. God's people had defiled themselves by worshiping an idol, and Moses knew that God would hold them accountable. They were closer than they knew to experiencing God's judgment.

What can you do to help others better understand the new covenant in Jesus Christ?

TO A FESTIVE GATHERING

(Read Hebrews 12:22-24.)

The new covenant on Mount Zion was marked by fellowship and joy. The name Zion (first mentioned in 2 Sam. 5:7) later came to be known as Jerusalem, David's capital city and the place where David's son, Solomon, built the Lord's temple (see 1 Kings 8:1). Mount Zion occupied an important place in the hearts of the people of Israel. In time, Mount Zion took on strong connections in the Old Testament to the coming Messiah (see Isa. 59:20; Mic. 4:7; Zech. 9:9).

Those readers of Hebrews with a background in Judaism would've been aware of the connection between Mount Zion and the new covenant. However, the writer of Hebrews didn't have in mind the earthly city of Jerusalem or its temple. Rather, he was referring to the Mount Zion Jesus went to prepare when He ascended to heaven (see John 14:2-3). In this heavenly community are countless angels, all of them serving the Lord in a festive gathering of sincere praise.

Where do your thoughts take you when you ponder what it will be like to see the Lord in heaven?

Although the community of believers may be different in a number of ways, they all have one trait in common—they belong to the fellowship of the firstborn. The writer also pointed attention to God who takes His rightful place on the throne as the final Judge who will hold all people everywhere accountable to Him. Believers who have welcomed Christ into their lives will stand before Him as the fellowship of the redeemed with the joy of having been made perfect in Christ.

How does the blending of God's majesty with His closeness impact the ways that you worship Him?

Now Jesus comes into view in the heavenly city. The Son of God took on human flesh and gave His life on the cross for us. With His death, Jesus paid the price for our salvation from sin. Therefore, He alone is qualified to be the Mediator between Holy God and sinful mankind.

The old covenant established at Mount Sinai centered in the law. The new covenant from Mount Zion centers in the gospel. Thanks to the new covenant, people who receive God's gift of salvation through Jesus Christ enjoy new life in Him. The new covenant is possible only through the blood of Christ sprinkled in the heavenly sanctuary.

The reference to Abel's blood was a reminder of the wicked act of Cain in murdering his brother (see Gen. 4:8-10). Abel's shed blood cried out for justice, and God heard it. Much more, however, the shed blood of Christ cried out for the forgiveness of sinners, and God accepted it. Cain's sin severed community; Christ's atoning blood restored it.

In what ways does your church look like a new covenant community composed of redeemed sinners?

Bible Skill:
Use a Bible atlas and Bible dictionary to locate and learn about places mentioned in Scripture.

Find the location of Mount Sinai in a Bible atlas. (Tip: Check the atlas index or search online.) Then use a Bible dictionary to learn more about Mount Sinai and Mount Zion (or Sion).

What are some significant facts about these two mountains that the writer of Hebrews emphasizes?

❯❯OBEY THE TEXT

Believers can joyfully approach the Father, putting aside fear and dread. This joy is seen in how believers relate to one another in community. The acceptance found in Christ can be offered to others willing to follow Him.

Based on this study, how would you describe the attitude a person should have when approaching God? What needs to change in your life for you to demonstrate this attitude to a greater degree?

In what ways can you help others understand that they can approach God with acceptance and joy?

How can your participation at your church's worship gatherings be a reflection of the truths of Hebrews 12:18-24?

How can you challenge other believers to build on the foundation of their faith? What role can you play in helping others mature in faith and produce spiritual fruit?

MENORIZE

"Since we are receiving a kingdom that cannot be shaken, let us hold on to grace. By it, we may serve God acceptably, with reverence and awe" (Hebrews 12:28).

Use the space provided to make observations and record prayer requests during the group experience for this session.

MY THOUGHTS

Record insights and questions from the group experience.

_____

_____

_____

_____

_____

_____

MY RESPONSE

Note specific ways you will put into practice the truth explored this week.

_____

_____

_____

_____

_____

MY PRAYERS

List specific prayer needs and answers to remember this week.

_____

_____

_____

_____

_____

LIVE OUT THE FAITH

Believers are to live to a higher standard.

❯ UNDERSTAND THE CONTEXT

PREPARE FOR YOUR GROUP EXPERIENCE WITH THE FOLLOWING PAGES.

In Hebrews 13 the writer introduced a wide range of ways that Christians are to live out the standard of holiness consistent with their salvation in Christ. As they put their faith in Christ to work, they were to be kind to strangers and prisoners. Moreover, the writer urged his readers to uphold God's standard of faithfulness in the marriage relationship.

Church members do well to follow the pattern of their Christian leaders in being faithful to Christ to the end. They can rest assured the Lord will never change (13:1-8).

But the writer didn't stop there. He moved on to give even greater attention to the place of Christ in his readers' lives as they walked by faith in Him. Evidently, they had encountered some false teachers who tried to lure them away from devotion to Jesus. The writer urged his readers to respond by focusing their attention all the more on God's grace demonstrated in Jesus' atoning death on the cross. The corpses of animals sacrificed on the Day of Atonement were taken outside the Israelite camp to be burned. Jesus was taken outside the walls of Jerusalem to be crucified. With Christ—outside the walls, so to speak—is where believers belong, serving together in a community formed by their common faith in Christ (13:9-17).

The ministry of intercessory prayer provided believers with a rewarding opportunity to put their faith in Christ to work. The writer demonstrated his confidence in prayer. As his readers prayed for him, they would see that he had a clear conscience about what he had written to them. In addition, he looked forward to being able to return to them in person (13:18-19).

> WE ARE RESPONSIBLE, WHETHER WE LIKE IT OR NOT, TO LIVE IN SUCH A WAY THAT PEOPLE WON'T BE DISAPPOINTED IN JESUS BECAUSE THE JESUS THEY SEE IS THE JESUS THEY SEE IN US.
> *David Jeremiah*

1 Let brotherly love continue.

2 Don't neglect to show hospitality, for by doing this some have welcomed angels as guests without knowing it.

3 Remember the prisoners, as though you were in prison with them, and the mistreated, as though you yourselves were suffering bodily.

4 Marriage must be respected by all, and the marriage bed kept undefiled, because God will judge immoral people and adulterers.

5 Your life should be free from the love of money. Be satisfied with what you have, for He Himself has said, I will never leave you or forsake you.

6 Therefore, we may boldly say: The Lord is my helper; I will not be afraid. What can man do to me?

7 Remember your leaders who have spoken God's word to you. As you carefully observe the outcome of their lives, imitate their faith.

8 Jesus Christ is the same yesterday, today, and forever.

Think About It

Observe all the action words used in this passage. Highlight the verbs that are commands.

Note one command you consistently thrive in obeying. Identify one you want to see get stronger in your Christian walk.

❯ EXPLORE THE TEXT

SHOW HOSPITALITY *(Read Hebrews 13:1-3.)*

After encouraging his readers to hold fast to their faith in Christ, the writer then urged them to nurture a vibrant, encouraging community of faith by intentionally practicing Christian love to brothers and sisters in Christ. Obeying the Great Commission (Matt. 28:19-20) is a demonstration of obedient love for a lost world that Jesus came to rescue. Obeying the Great Commandments (Matt. 22:37-39) is a demonstration of genuine love for God and for God's redeemed people, the community of faith.

How can you show God's love to other believers?

*How can you show God's love to unbelievers
in your neighborhood?*

In New Testament times the stranger might be a person traveling on a long journey. Hospitality called for believers to take travelers in for the night, to feed them, and to provide protection from the elements and other dangers. In other words, they were to treat strangers like family members. One might never know when the traveler, as in Abraham's example (see Gen. 18:1-10), was a messenger of God.

Most prisons in biblical times had no obligation to provide even the basic needs of prisoners—food, clothing, and medical care (such as it might have been). These basics often had to be provided by a prisoner's family or friends. The prisoners mentioned in this verse perhaps were believers who had been jailed as a result of their confession of Christ. Regardless, the community of faith was not to forget them.

In what ways can you practice hospitality to strangers?

RESPECT MARRIAGE *(Read Hebrews 13:4.)*

In many pagan cultures, faithfulness in marriage didn't seem to matter very much. For Christians, however, marriage needed to be viewed as a precious treasure. God sanctified marriage, and He intended for His people to honor it (see Gen. 2:24; Ex. 20:14; Mal. 2:14-15). Likewise, Jesus affirmed God's standard for marriage and taught His disciples to honor it (see Mark 10:6-9).

Husbands and wives who follow Christ are under obligation to be faithful to each other. The "marriage bed" refers in particular to the intimacy of the marriage relationship. The apostle Paul strongly warned the believers living in Corinth in that day to reject the city's gross idolatry of sexual immorality (see 1 Cor. 6:15-20). Because we serve a pure, holy God, we are to be holy also.

Because God created and sanctified the marriage relationship, those who ignore or devalue it should expect God to hold them accountable for upholding His marriage standards. For this reason, Christians are to resist all temptations of sexual immorality.

What can you do to uphold God's standard for marriage? In what ways can the church help married couples strengthen their relationships?

SECURITY IN GOD *(Read Hebrews 13:5-6.)*

Immorality and adultery have a close connection to greed and covetousness. In God's economy, we as believers earn money so that we can use it to serve the Lord. We love Him with all our hearts, and we want to use the money we earn in ways that please Him.

Ultimately, money will let us down. Every day, we must face the possibility that someone may steal it, inflation might devalue it, or we could lose it. But the Lord will never let us down or forsake us.

Our confidence in the Lord makes us bold as we face the challenges life brings. The Lord will help His people at every turn (see Ps. 118:6). Because we trust Him, we believe He will be faithful to provide what money can't buy. Our certainty in His faithfulness pushes fear aside and prompts us to pledge that we won't be afraid when we face uncertainties.

In your own life, how has being content in the Lord proved more worthy than having lots of money?

IMITATE PROVEN LEADERS *(Read Hebrews 13:7-8.)*

Effective Christian leadership is vital for the community of faith (see Heb. 13:7,17,24). The writer was particularly interested in reminding his readers of those leaders who had faithfully guided believers to live out God's Word. Included in that select group were preachers who had shared the gospel and people who became pastors to them, teaching the truths of Scripture by precept and example.

We who are part of the community of faith today also need to remember and honor the Christian leaders who have made a difference in our lives. As we carefully observe their lives, we gain important insights about serving the Lord and the motivation to do so. They encourage us by their examples to finish well. They urge us to stand firm and remain faithful to the Lord from start to finish in the race of faith.

Who are some of your heroes of faith in the Lord?

How do they inspire you to remain faithful to Christ?

Faithful Christian leaders show us by example how to walk by faith in the Lord. However, they cannot stay with us forever. They live and die. Like all of us in this life on earth, they are, as it were, here today and gone tomorrow. No matter how well they live, in time their journey of faith will come to an end. However, Jesus never leaves His people. His presence through the Holy Spirit is with us forever.

The writer included two names in this verse by which to identify the Lord. He referred to Him as Jesus and as Christ. He used the two names together in this way in two previous places in his letter (see 10:10; 13:8). The name *Jesus* calls to mind everything about the Savior from His incarnation (birth) to His death and resurrection. Jesus fully took on human nature. At the same time, Jesus was God in the flesh. The name *Christ* emphasizes His fully divine nature.

Taken together, these two precious names help us understand the absolute faithfulness of Jesus Christ to the community of faith. He will never leave us, and His journey with us will never come to an end. We can trust Him to be the same Savior and Lord, no matter how much our circumstances may change.

In what ways have you experienced the presence of Jesus Christ in your life this week?

Bible Skill:
Take seriously all biblical commands for Christian living.

Identify at least six biblical commands for Christian living found in Hebrews 13:1-8. Express them as brief, positive imperatives. (Example: "Love other Christians," v. 1) Develop a "path of obedience" for each imperative. That is, think of reasons God gave these commands.

Consider damage that might be caused by ignoring them and benefits generated by obeying them. Identify at least one way you will intentionally put the commands into practice.

❯ OBEY THE TEXT

The ways that believers treat one another demonstrate the depth to which they understand the gospel. Believers are characterized by respect for marriage. God's presence influences how believers treat others, especially the down and out. Faithful Christian leaders serve as examples to the community of faith.

Examine your relationships with others in your Bible study group. What actions do you need to take to restore, strengthen, or develop relationships?

What actions can you take to affirm biblical marriage? How can you do so in a way that demonstrates God's standards in a caring way?

How can you pass your faith on to the next generation? Who is one person you can invest in spiritually during the days ahead, and how?

MEMORIZE

"Jesus Christ is the same yesterday, today, and forever" (Hebrews 13:8).

Use the space provided to make observations and record prayer requests during the group experience for this session.

MY THOUGHTS

Record insights and questions from the group experience.

_____
_____
_____
_____
_____
_____

MY RESPONSE

Note specific ways you will put into practice the truth explored this week.

_____
_____
_____
_____
_____
_____

MY PRAYERS

List specific prayer needs and answers to remember this week.

_____
_____
_____
_____
_____
_____

❯ GETTING STARTED

OPTIONS TO BEGIN: **Choose one of the following to begin your group discussion:**

WEEKLY QUOTE DISCUSSION STARTER: "The Old Covenant spoke outwardly to the inward man, but what was needed was something that could speak inwardly to the outward man. The New Covenant was given to do just that."—DAVID JEREMIAH

[handwritten: 1st part man has no part in anything—the Priest does it all]

> What is your initial response to this week's quote? *[handwritten: New Christ wrote on his heart — to look in word]*

> What is the relationship between behavior and character? *[handwritten: Your behavior builds character (defined by what you do)]*

CREATIVE ACTIVITY: Prior to the group gathering, prepare a pen and notepad. Explain that group members will play a game that is a hybrid of telephone and pictionary. Provide the category: movie titles. Clarify that people will silently pass a notepad and alternate between drawing a picture of or writing words for whatever they see; if they are shown a picture, they write a title and if they are shown a title, they draw a picture. Individuals are only allowed to see the paper of the person immediately before them in the circle before turning the page. Allow 20 seconds per turn before telling the person to pass the pad and pen. Start the game by writing a movie title and handing the pad to the first person. When the pad has circled back to you, reveal the progression of drawings and titles, starting with what you provided. Use the following questions to launch the group discussion:

> How well did people interpret and reproduce what they were given? How did things break down over time? Ultimately, who was the only person who could correct the situation?

> How have you personally experienced change over time?

❯ UNDERSTAND THE CONTEXT

PROVIDE BACKGROUND: Briefly bring all group members up to speed on the Book of Hebrews by pointing out the major themes of the book as whole and any information or ideas that will help your group members explore Hebrews 8:1-13, specifically. Then, to personally connect today's context with the original context, ask the following questions:

> Why was the superiority of Jesus so important for the original Christians? *[handwritten: Jesus replaced the law of the Jewish people]*

> What traditions and worldviews tend to most influence our own lives today (religious, philosophical, family, cultural, political)?

❯ EXPLORE THE TEXT

READ THE BIBLE: Ask for a volunteer to read aloud Hebrews 8:1-13.

DISCUSS: Use the following questions to unpack your group members' initial reactions to the text.

> *Verse 10*
> What do you like best about these verses? What questions do you have?

> What was the significance of the sanctuary and tabernacle in biblical history?

> *Promises of God*
> What is a covenant? And what does it reveal about the character of God—a holy, sovereign, and superior God—that He made covenant relationship possible? *His love for mankind*

> Verse 7 clarifies that a second covenant was necessary. Was fault found with the first covenant and therefore with God, or were the people to blame? What does that reveal about grace? *God* *could have put us all to death - but Grace*
> *The people got away from it.*

> What are the specific qualities of the new covenant detailed in verses 8-13? What are the implications of each? *write new laws on our heart & mind, He will be our God and we will be his people*

NOTE: Provide ample time for group members to share responses and questions about the text. Don't feel pressured to prioritize the printed agenda over your group members' personal experiences. If time allows, discuss responses to the questions in the reading.

❯ OBEY THE TEXT

RESPOND: Foster an environment of openness and action. Help individuals apply biblical truth to specific areas of personal thought, attitude, and/or behavior.

> How will your covenant relationship with Christ transform your daily life this week?

> What will you do to live in the freedom and forgiveness Christ has provided?

> What is it that nobody has to tell you—you just know God has put it in your heart— that you need to do as a response to His mercy?

PRAY: Conclude with prayer. Using Hebrews 8 as a guide, thank God for His mercy in forgiving our sins—never again remembering them—and entering into covenant relationship with us through Jesus. Ask Him to fill the hearts and minds of everyone in your group with His truth and with His Spirit for belief and obedience.

For helps on how to use *Explore the Bible,* tips on how to better lead groups, or additional ideas for leading, visit www.ministrygrid.com/web/ExploreTheBible.

❯ GETTING STARTED

OPTIONS TO BEGIN: Choose one of the following to begin your group discussion:

WEEKLY QUOTE DISCUSSION STARTER: "Only by being both deity and humanity could Jesus Christ bridge the gap between where we are and where God is. Without Jesus Christ, there is no hope of any of us ever having a relationship with the Holy God."—DAVID JEREMIAH

> ❯ What is your initial response to this week's quote?

> ❯ When did you first recognize your need for Christ, personally? Share a brief story about how you came to see your hopelessness without Christ and the hope only He could offer.

CREATIVE ACTIVITY: Prior to the group gathering, find a video clip from a movie or TV show of a person receiving a surprisingly large inheritance. If video is not convenient, find examples of famous, extravagant, or unusual last wills and testaments (eg. Napoleon ordered his head shaved and hair passed out to friends, Leona Helmsley left $12 million to her dog and billions to charity but nothing to her children, Ted Williams desired to be cryogenically frozen in the chance that he could later be thawed and live in the future). Use the following questions to start the group discussion:

> ❯ Have any of you or your families ever received something of sentimental or monetary value as an inheritance? If so, what was it?

> ❯ How can a gift be used to change someone's life for the better?

❯ UNDERSTAND THE CONTEXT

PROVIDE BACKGROUND: Briefly introduce group members to any information or ideas that will help everyone explore Hebrews 9:11-15. Then, to personally connect today's context with the original context, ask the following questions:

> ❯ What had to happen to transfer blessings through sacrifice or a final will?

> ❯ What benefits do we receive from the death of Jesus? Unlike most sacrifices and wills, what benefit do we also receive from a relationship with a resurrected and living Savior?

❯ EXPLORE THE TEXT

READ THE BIBLE: Ask for a volunteer to read aloud Hebrews 9:11-15.

DISCUSS: Use the following questions to unpack your group members' initial reactions to the text.

> What do you like best about these verses? What questions do you have?

Christ is the Mediator of a new cov. v. 15

> Why was sacrifice necessary in relating to God?

Sacrifice was necessary for forgiveness from God

> How was Jesus both the perfect priest and sacrifice?

Jesus went into the inner sacuary bc he was sinless — his crucifixion was good before God bc he was sinl.

> What is the significance of the phrase "once for all" in verse 12?

Jesus entered the inner sactuary by his own blood.

> Explain the words *promise, eternal inheritance,* and *redemption* in verse 15.

promise - God covenant, everlasting life, sinner = ask for redemption

NOTE: Provide ample time for group members to share responses and questions about the text. Don't feel pressured to prioritize the printed agenda over your group members' personal experiences. If time allows, discuss responses to the questions in the reading.

❯ OBEY THE TEXT

RESPOND: Foster an environment of openness and action. Help individuals apply biblical truth to specific areas of personal thought, attitude, and/or behavior.

> How will the perfect sacrifice of Jesus—shedding His own blood for you and for others— change your thoughts, attitudes, and actions this week?

> What will you do to keep this sacrifice in the front of your heart and mind?

PRAY: Conclude with prayer. Spend time praising God for the invaluable blessings He has so generously given in this life and for eternity. Thank Him for the sacrifice of Jesus. Ask for His help in living humbly and sacrificially in order to share the inheritance of Christ with all of God's people.

❯ GETTING STARTED

OPTIONS TO BEGIN: Choose one of the following to begin your group discussion:

WEEKLY QUOTE DISCUSSION STARTER: "For the unbeliever, seeing is believing. For the believer, believing is seeing."—DAVID JEREMIAH

> ❯ What is your initial response to this week's quote?

> ❯ When have you had to do something blindly, trusting that it was right even though you couldn't see everything? How did it prove to be the right thing?

CREATIVE ACTIVITY: Prior to the group gathering, search for and save "optical illusions" to display either on a screen or printed on paper. Use the following questions to launch the group discussion:

> ❯ How can our sight be deceptive?

> ❯ What can we not see, even though we know it is real and experience it in other ways?

> ❯ How is living by faith not a matter of wishful thinking with no basis in reality, but rather a matter of trusting realities we cannot see?

❯ UNDERSTAND THE CONTEXT

PROVIDE BACKGROUND: Briefly introduce group members to any information or ideas that will help everyone explore Hebrews 11:1-7. Then, to personally connect today's context with the original context, ask the following questions:

> ❯ Why was it important for the original audience of the Book of Hebrews to have faith defined and exemplified?

> ❯ Who are you looking to as an example of faith? Who might be looking to you?

❯ EXPLORE THE TEXT

READ THE BIBLE: Ask for a volunteer to read aloud Hebrews 11:1-7.

DISCUSS: Use the following questions to unpack your group members' initial reactions to the text.

> What do you like best about these verses? What questions do you have?

> After reading this, how would you say the Bible defines faith?

> What is the approval, pleasure, and reward of God?

> What is the significance of the examples provided in these verses, both natural and historical?

NOTE: Provide ample time for group members to share responses and questions about the text. Don't feel pressured to prioritize the printed agenda over your group members' personal experiences. If time allows, discuss responses to the questions in the reading.

❯ OBEY THE TEXT

RESPOND: Foster an environment of openness and action. Help individuals apply biblical truth to specific areas of personal thought, attitude, and/or behavior.

> Honestly, do you desire to please God and to draw near to Him? If so, what are you doing to try to please Him and to draw nearer to Him? If not, why is His approval not important?

> What are you facing that you don't understand? What step of faith do you need to make?

PRAY: Conclude with prayer. Ask God to help everyone live by faith, seeking to live for His approval, not for their own limited understanding. Pray that group members would be living examples of faithfulness and would experience the pleasure of God as they draw closer to Him.

❯ GETTING STARTED

OPTIONS TO BEGIN: Choose one of the following to begin your group discussion:

WEEKLY QUOTE DISCUSSION STARTER: "Life is about doing hard things that you don't want to do because you believe the result of doing those hard things is going to create great joy and great good—not only for you and for others, but most of all for the glory of the Lord Jesus Christ."
—DAVID JEREMIAH

> ❯ What is your initial response to this week's quote?

> ❯ What do our choices reveal about what we ultimately value as most desirable?

CREATIVE ACTIVITY: Prior to the group gathering, secure plastic spoons to the bottom of a cooler or deep bowl and fill it with ice. Begin scooping ice cream into bowls as people arrive (or use forks and another dessert or snack item). Once everyone has arrived, explain that a volunteer is needed to get the utensils for everyone, but they are stuck inside the ice chest. After someone volunteers and everyone has their treat, use the following questions to launch the group discussion:

> ❯ What did people's responses to the dilemma reveal?

> ❯ When have you endured an uncomfortable, inconvenient, or even painful situation in order to gain something personally and/or for others?

❯ UNDERSTAND THE CONTEXT

PROVIDE BACKGROUND: Briefly introduce group members to any information or ideas that will help everyone explore Hebrews 12:1-7. Then, to personally connect today's context with the original context, ask the following questions:

> ❯ Today's passage starts with the word *therefore*, meaning it is a conclusion based on what has been discussed previously. So let's review. What did we discuss last time? And what pressures did first century Christians have to endure?

> ❯ How are these pressures similar today? What other stresses might wear us out today?

❯ EXPLORE THE TEXT

READ THE BIBLE: Ask for a volunteer to read aloud Hebrews 12:1-7.

DISCUSS: Use the following questions to unpack your group members' initial reactions to the text.

- ❯ What do you like best about these verses? What questions do you have?

- ❯ Who are the great cloud of witnesses? What is their function in this text?

- ❯ What specific truths are revealed about Jesus in these verses?

- ❯ What perspective do these verses offer regarding joy? Regarding suffering? How does this change or encourage your approach to holiness and spiritual growth?

NOTE: Provide ample time for group members to share responses and questions about the text. Don't feel pressured to prioritize the printed agenda over your group members' personal experiences. If time allows, discuss responses to the questions in the reading.

❯ OBEY THE TEXT

RESPOND: Foster an environment of openness and action. Help individuals apply biblical truth to specific areas of personal thought, attitude, and/or behavior.

- ❯ What weight or sin most easily ensnares you?

- ❯ What specific step will you take to lay that aside in order to more freely follow Christ?

- ❯ How can we be a cloud of witnesses to help you endure in freedom and faithfulness?

PRAY: Conclude with prayer. Explain that you will provide an instruction to guide a minute for everyone to silently reflect and pray. Encourage everyone to identify specific sin that is tripping them up—getting in the way of their spiritual progress as a follower of Christ. Then prompt everyone to surrender that to Christ—turning away from it in confession and repentance. Next direct everyone to now identify suffering in their lives. Finally, ask everyone to pray for eyes to see how a loving heavenly Father may be disciplining them in order to grow them to maturity. Pray for everyone to focus on the joy of Christ as they endure in their daily walk following Him.

❱ GETTING STARTED

OPTIONS TO BEGIN: **Choose one of the following to begin your group discussion:**

WEEKLY QUOTE DISCUSSION STARTER: "Mount Sinai gave the law that only the cross could satisfy."—DAVID JEREMIAH

> ❱ What is your initial response to this week's quote? *You would have to be perfect to not sin. That is why Jesus died for our sin*

> ❱ What purpose does law serve in our world? What would happen if judgments did not uphold the penalty for breaking the law? *People would break the law all the time chaos*

CREATIVE ACTIVITY: If your members enjoy eating during your group time, prepare at least two different sweets/snacks for everyone to taste. Have people think about how they would explain the flavors to someone. If food is not preferable, pair people up with different favorite hobbies and have a few volunteers explain the similarities and differences to the group. Then use the following questions to launch the group discussion:

> ❱ How is comparing similarities a helpful way to explain and understand something? How is contrasting differences helpful?

> ❱ When has comparing and contrasting truth about God to something you were more familiar with helped you better understand or apply your understanding?

❱ UNDERSTAND THE CONTEXT

PROVIDE BACKGROUND: Briefly introduce group members to any information or ideas that will help everyone explore Hebrews 12:18-24. Then, to personally connect today's context with the original context, ask the following questions:

> ❱ What do you know about the Ten Commandments and their origin? *Mt Sinai terrified everyone. Moses was terrified to go up it*

> ❱ The commandments God gave to Moses on Mount Sinai represent a summary of the law on how humanity is to relate to God and to one another—it was the standard for the ancient Hebrew community. No matter how much people today say we should respect and keep the commandments, can we even say all ten? Has anyone in history perfectly kept just those ten? *No*

Where was Mt. Sinai — is it there today?

EXPLORE THE TEXT

READ THE BIBLE: Ask for a volunteer to read aloud Hebrews 12:18-24.

DISCUSS: Use the following questions to unpack your group members' initial reactions to the text.

> What do you like best about these verses? What questions do you have?

Mt. Zion, Jerusalem, the city of the living God.

> What does the seriousness of this historical description reveal about God? (See 18-21)

Cannot bear Mt. Sinai — what would happen if refuse God.

> What does the change in tone, from seriousness to celebration reveal about the character of God's new community of people? (See 22-24.)

What would happen if you accept God.

> What similarities exist throughout history regarding God's people? What difference has the Book of Hebrews revealed for people now in Christ?

Keep your faith in God for what can man do to you? Faith. Do good. Share with others.

> How would you explain the phrase "made perfect" in verse 23?

Mt. Zion is heaven — spirits be righteous in his eyes Made perfect. Pray constantly.

NOTE: Provide ample time for group members to share responses and questions about the text. Don't feel pressured to prioritize the printed agenda over your group members' personal experiences. If time allows, discuss responses to the questions in the reading.

OBEY THE TEXT

RESPOND: Foster an environment of openness and action. Help individuals apply biblical truth to specific areas of personal thought, attitude, and/or behavior.

> How will you take more seriously the holiness of God?

> What will you do this week because you have been declared perfect before a righteous Judge?

> Who will you talk to this week, comparing and contrasting what they know to the amazing truth of Jesus and life with Him in heaven? Will you invite them to experience your new community, joining you for worship and/or small group?

PRAY: Conclude with prayer. Encourage group members to voice prayers of gratitude that God has brought them near through Christ. Encourage them to also express specific gratitude for the community of faith, including the people in this group. You may want to help lead in this prayer, naming things about the individuals and the collective group that have blessed you.

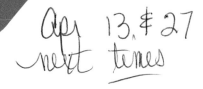
apr 13, & 27 next times

GETTING STARTED

OPTIONS TO BEGIN: Choose one of the following to begin your group discussion:

WEEKLY QUOTE DISCUSSION STARTER: "We are responsible, whether we like it or not, to live in such a way that people won't be disappointed in Jesus because the Jesus they see is the Jesus they see in us."—DAVID JEREMIAH

> What is your initial response to this week's quote? *Comfort & excitment*

> How has your picture of Jesus changed over time (even over the weeks in this group/study)? *It has not changed.*

> If someone were to look at your life, where might they get the wrong idea about Jesus? *Not using talents for spreading his word enough.*

CREATIVE ACTIVITY: Prior to the group gathering, gather several images of popular brands. (For example: Mac, PC, Android logos or ads, or others are often blatant in personifying a type or image. Other brands may be more relevant for your group.) Show or name the various brand logos or ads, then use the following questions to launch the group discussion:

> What brands (products/services/stores) elicit a positive reaction for you? Negative? Why?

> How might people have a negative image of Jesus and His people—the church? As His representatives and bearing His image, what positive experiences have you had worth sharing with the world? *Appeal to Heaven flag – American flag Household spiritual decor*

UNDERSTAND THE CONTEXT

PROVIDE BACKGROUND: Briefly introduce group members to any information or ideas that will help everyone explore Hebrews 13:1-8. Then, to personally connect today's context with the original context, ask the following questions:

> Why would the Book of Hebrews end with practical instructions after 12 chapters of deep theological focus? *Brought deep thoughts to broad terms so easier*

> Is there a benefit of learning about the superiority of Christ but not living any differently from those who have no saving relationship with Him? Explain. *No benefit. Truely knowing Jesus is life changing*

EXPLORE THE TEXT

READ THE BIBLE: Ask for a volunteer to read aloud Hebrews13:1-8.

DISCUSS: Use the following questions to unpack your group members' initial reactions to the text.

> What do you like best about these verses? What questions do you have?
> *Jesus is telling you how to live to best be like him.*

> How is hospitality a spiritual act? How is respecting authority a spiritual act?
> *Friendly & Respectful — follows Bible teaching*

> How is marriage to be a picture of the gospel and Christian faith?
> *Man & Woman become ONE — pray / go to church / READ the Bible*

> How do attitudes toward money relate to an understanding of the superiority of Christ?
> *Give your tithe first, then pay other things. Follow him & he will bless you.*

> What encouragement exists knowing that Jesus will "never leave you or forsake you" and that He "is the same yesterday, today, and forever"? *excitement, calm, and Love*

NOTE: Provide ample time for group members to share responses and questions about the text. Don't feel pressured to prioritize the printed agenda over your group members' personal experiences. If time allows, discuss responses to the questions in the reading.

OBEY THE TEXT

RESPOND: Foster an environment of openness and action. Help individuals apply biblical truth to specific areas of personal thought, attitude, and/or behavior.

> Looking back over this list in 13:1-8 of practical applications for the Book of Hebrews, what can you specifically do this week to live out the faith? *Live like Jesus would*

> How will you be different after studying the Book of Hebrews?

> Who in your life would benefit from time like this in God's Word and community with brothers and sisters in Christ? What will you do to model gospel truths and/or invite others to join you in whatever God leads you to next?

PRAY: Conclude with prayer. Pray that everyone would be encouraged, remember what they have learned and experienced, and that it would change their day-to-day lives. Emphasize our need to persevere in putting into practice what we know to be true because Jesus is worthy of our lives.

❯TIPS FOR LEADING A GROUP

PRAYERFULLY PREPARE

Prepare for each session by—

> ❯ **reviewing the weekly material and group questions ahead of time;**

> ❯ **praying for each person in the group.**

Ask the Holy Spirit to work through you and the group discussion to help people take steps toward Jesus each week as directed by God's Word.

MINIMIZE DISTRACTIONS

Create a comfortable environment. If group members are uncomfortable, they'll be distracted and therefore not engaged in the group experience. Plan ahead by taking into consideration—

> ❯ **seating;**

> ❯ **temperature;**

> ❯ **lighting;**

> ❯ **food or drink;**

> ❯ **surrounding noise;**

> ❯ **general cleanliness (put pets away if meeting in a home).**

At best, thoughtfulness and hospitality show guests and group members they're welcome and valued in whatever environment you choose to gather. At worst, people may never notice your effort, but they're also not distracted. Do everything in your ability to help people focus on what's most important: connecting with God, with the Bible, and with others.

INCLUDE OTHERS

Your goal is to foster a community in which people are welcome just as they are but encouraged to grow spiritually. Always be aware of opportunities to—

> ❯ **invite** new people to join your group;

> ❯ **include** any people who visit the group.

An inexpensive way to make first-time guests feel welcome or to invite people to get involved is to give them their own copies of this Bible-study book.

ENCOURAGE DISCUSSION

A good small group has the following characteristics.

> **Everyone participates.** Encourage everyone to ask questions, share responses, or read aloud.

> **No one dominates—not even the leader.** Be sure what you say takes up less than half of your time together as a group. Politely redirect discussion if anyone dominates.

> **Nobody is rushed through questions.** Don't feel that a moment of silence is a bad thing. People often need time to think about their responses to questions they've just heard or to gain courage to share what God is stirring in their hearts.

> **Input is affirmed and followed up.** Make sure you point out something true or helpful in a response. Don't just move on. Build personal connections with follow-up questions, asking how other people have experienced similar things or how a truth has shaped their understanding of God and the Scripture you're studying. People are less likely to speak up if they fear that you don't actually want to hear their answers or that you're looking for only a certain answer.

> **God and His Word are central.** Opinions and experiences can be helpful, but God has given us the truth. Trust Scripture to be the authority and God's Spirit to work in people's lives. You can't change anyone, but God can. Continually point people to the Word and to active steps of faith.

KEEP CONNECTING

Think of ways to connect with members during the week. Participation during the session is always improved when members spend time connecting with one another away from the session. The more people are comfortable with and involved in one another's lives, the more they'll look forward to being together. When people move beyond being friendly and in the same group to truly being friends who form a community, they come to each session eager to engage instead of merely attending.

Encourage group members with thoughts, commitments, or questions from the session by connecting through—

> emails;
> texts;
> social media.

When possible, build deeper friendships by planning or spontaneously inviting group members to join you outside your regularly scheduled group time for—

> meals;
> fun activities;
> projects around your home, church, or community.

❯ GROUP CONTACT INFORMATION

Name _____ Number _____
Email _____

Name _____ Number _____
Email _____

Name _____ Number _____
Email _____

Name _____ Number _____
Email _____

Name _____ Number _____
Email _____

Name _____ Number _____
Email _____

Name _____ Number _____
Email _____

Name _____ Number _____
Email _____

Name _____ Number _____
Email _____

Name _____ Number _____
Email _____

Name _____ Number _____
Email _____